YOUNG, FRUITFUL & SINGLE

BEING WHO GOD WANTS YOU TO BE BEFORE THE RING

I0149341

TAYLOR C. LIDDELL

FOREWORD WRITTEN BY PARYS D. LIDDELL, SR.

Young, Fruitful & Single: Being Who God Wants You to Be Before the Ring.

© 2018 Taylor Ciara Liddell

All rights reserved. Except in the case of brief quotations in critical reviews or articles, no part of this book may be reproduced or transmitted in any form or by any means be it electronic, mechanical, photocopy, scanning, recording, information storage and retrieval systems or other without expressed written consent of the publisher/author.

Any Internet addresses, phone numbers or company or product information printed in the book are offered as a resource and are not in any way intended to act as, suggest or imply endorsement of this book.

All scripture quotations and references are from:

THE HOLY BIBLE, NEW INTERNATIONAL VERSION®, NIV® Copyright © 1973, 1978, 1984, 2011 by Biblica, Inc.® Used by permission. All rights reserved worldwide.

THE HOLY BIBLE, NEW INTERNATIONAL VERSION®, NIV® Copyright © 1973, 1978, 1984 by International Bible Society. Used by permission of Zondervan. All rights reserved.

ISBN: 978-0-692-13292-0
LCCN: 2018907342

Printed in the United States of America

This book will be eternally dedicated to the inspiration behind my words; my daily motivator, my biggest fan, my best friend and life partner, my husband, Parys D. Liddell, Sr. Thank you for believing in me and trusting me. Our lives are God's canvas and what a BEAUTIFUL mural He's creating. I love you, boo!

<u>Foreword</u>

"He who heeds discipline shows the way to life, but whoever ignores correction leads others astray." – Proverbs 10:17 NIV

Proverbs is a book you can always turn to for sound wisdom. Discipline is one of those words that is much easier said than done. We all lack it in some area of our life whether it be in finances, love or healthy living. Sometimes it's the only thing in the way of us being our best selves. Lacking discipline has cost me many opportunities and relationships in the past but sometimes the only way to grow through something is to learn the hard way. I'm so thankful for God's mercy and grace that it didn't cost me to miss out on meeting my amazing wife.

Taylor understands the true meaning *discipline* beyond the definition. *Young, Fruitful & Single: Being*

Who God Wants You to Be Before the Ring is a book written from both personal experiences and with the wisdom gained through revelation. Being single is not a label to be ashamed of but instead a journey you can face with enthusiasm. Each page will challenge your thinking and open your eyes to what is essential to obtain before seeking to be married. Being intentional is the first step to achieve anything you want and since you're reading this book you are on the right track!

Dear, I'm so thankful that your discipline in finding your husband allowed our paths to cross. I'm honored that you would include my words in your charge.

All my love,

Parys D. Liddell, Sr

Table of Contents

Introduction

Introduction

God is a good God. Even when times are bad, He is still good. And, He will never give you more than you can handle. These are the things that we know; the things that we hear very often in the church. He didn't put the late fee on that bill because He knew your finances couldn't handle it. He didn't allow you to run out of gas because He knew that you couldn't be late for work, meaning your job couldn't handle it. And, also, He hasn't given you the person whom you've been praying for simply because you cannot handle it...YET! Now, this doesn't mean you won't *ever* be ready or that God is just outright saying "NO!" He is simply saying "not yet!"

In grade school, we had spelling tests at the end of every week and the teacher would help us prepare so that by Friday we were ready. Bottom line: we couldn't be ready if we didn't prepare. And, just like my old teacher, God is right alongside us, giving us ways to improve our character and lessons to help prepare you for the true test of marriage. Now, I know that some women specifically believe that they do not even want to be married. To you ladies, I say this: Genesis 3:16 NIV says "...*Your desire will be for your husband*..." In addition to the curse of child labor pains, as designed by God, *every* woman will have an innate desire to marry and have a husband to follow. This is why little girls plan their weddings from birth - it's already in them! So, if you have yet to experience the desire to be married, it will surely come at an eventual time.

Aside from that scripture, human nature also causes us to long for a love to share our good and bad times with. It is especially difficult when we see our friends all going off to get married and start their families. And then you begin to think that maybe God forgot about you in the love department. But it is not until we fully understand and apply what God's definition of love is that we can *begin* to be ready (notice I didn't say 100% ready). Truth is, you're never going to be 100% ready for something as unpredictable as marriage but as much preparation as possible can carry you a long way.

Imagine this: You are gainfully employed, financially responsible, you maintain a respectable social status & you have a healthy relationship with The Lord. You are also (dare I say, the "S" word) SINGLE.

And because of your attributes, you simply cannot understand WHY! You look at everybody else and amid their happiness and togetherness...there's you, with your loneliness and sulking. But, is this period as bad as your impatience makes you to believe? Isolation is a mechanism that I learned about God. It is where He will place you before the elevation. It's a time where He provides you with plenty of opportunity to discover more about first, Him and then self. Unfortunately, some are much too wrapped up in their own desires of a relationship that they sail right past God's plans and walk right into their plans, ending up with some no-good mate with no clue of who they even are themselves!

There is no thought worse than being in a marriage with someone who God did not design to be

YOUR spouse. The butt-naked truth is this: when you place yourself outside of God's Will, that means you are fighting, trying, resenting and crying over *someone else's* husband or wife. Take a moment to think about this; when you entangle yourself with a person who God did not intend to be for you, you are essentially entangling yourself with another person's spouse; someone who God did not set aside for you but for another person. But at least you aren't single, anymore right? WRONG! Seek to be who and what God has called for you to be FIRST (Matthew 6:33 NIV). Your friends and colleagues are all involved but not you because the plans that God has designed your life for are far more extensive than that of your friends and colleagues. Maybe you were meant to go a bit further in life and He knows that a premature mate will distract you. God is a jealous god (Deuteronomy 4:24 NIV) and He gives each of us a divine purpose so that we can keep busy on Earth while giving Him the glory. Now, do you *really* think He is going to give you a man or woman to preoccupy your time instead of working in your purpose and giving Him His rightful glory? But how do you get to the point of giving Him His rightful glory and being who He's called you to be *before* the ring?

As a young person, we must first develop and then define who He has purposed us to be. Nothing can come before this step because it lies the foundation for everything else that you will ever become in your entire life.

By no means, do I claim to be a relationship expert or life coach. I do not think that I have the best method of achieving partnership but I know what worked for me in my life. I have seen several of my high school friends spiral downward in their quest for true love and feel that I have some knowledge that is worth sharing with my generation to keep this from continuing to happen. Hopefully, each chapter is as easy for you to read as they were for me to write them. This book was especially written with every young person in mind because I was once that very young person to whom I am writing.

Each chapter will demonstrate what being single means to God *and* how much it means to God and also, how much of a good thing it can be! You haven't been overlooked. You haven't been forgotten. And He hears every one of those prayers you pray out of loneliness, anger or frustration. But, the truth is that you cannot feel lonely, angry or frustrated until you think about how He must feel. He has this child that He has blessed tremendously but this child is too impatient...too stubborn...to wait for Him to give them a mate. I've done it. You've done it. If nobody has told you, I will: if you haven't waited on God, you're settling. Period. He's called you to a much higher ground but just like a hot air balloon you can never rise without having first been ignited by a flame!

Chapter 1

Finding Your Flame

Often, you hear men and women saying, "I know I'm a good catch!" and their reasons are because they have a good job, they learned how to fry chicken and can work a washing machine. But, what *is* a good woman or a good man? Take a minute to write down what makes you "good":

_____

_____

_____

Look at the list you just made. Per *you*, this is what makes you a "good" potential spouse. But, who are all the things you've listed good for? I will tell you who. YOU! *You* assessed *yourself* based on the qualities and attributes that *you think* anyone would want to have in a mate and *you* concluded that you are good because of these things. So now…you can marry yourself and live happily ever after! Did you catch that? With carnal (fleshly, physical) thinking, what makes a person good is simple. But in the spirit, things are a bit more complex. A good woman to any man is what that particular man needs for his woman to be (and vice versa). What does this mean, Taylor? If you come across a man who loves to dine out 7 days a week, has a six-figure salary and has been washing his own clothes since college, then your home-fried chicken, good job and washing skills won't mean much to him. But, someone who values and adjusts to what he loves and needs will mean the world to him. Now, that's not to say that you should lose all of your qualities because in our microwavable society where everything is done quick and in a hurry, the truth is that being able to work, cook and clean is commendable and necessary, especially if your union produces children. However, the drive home point here is to remind you that for men and women alike, you do not know what will be good for a potential spouse until you meet them, court them and find out what speaks to their true interests.

As a pre-medical student, there is this thing called a "gap year (or years), where instead of matriculating right into medical school from being an undergraduate student, you take the time in between to further develop as a person. This could mean anything from taking a few extra classes to boost your GPA or just traveling the world before you get knee-deep in the swampy waters of studying medicine. Based on my observations and conversations I've had with employers, it is often thought that the life experience that comes with a gap year creates a more well-rounded physician. And, this is not to take away from the doctor who was able to go right into medical school in any way.

For late bloomers (like myself), sometimes, a little extra time can add a bit more seasoning and real-life experience to your knowledge and produce wisdom (which is knowledge in action). In this context, while knowledge is knowing that you have to be a good person to make a marriage work, wisdom is understanding that your goodness is tailor-made to the mate that God gives you.

This reminds me of the saying "what's good for the goose isn't always good for the gander." The kind of "good" that we once were may not be "good" enough for who we are to become. Nine times out of ten, our earlier relationships are chosen by us with little to no input from the Holy Spirit. With that in mind, do you think who you were in your very first (real) relationship could have withstood your most recent relationship? Probably not. I know mine couldn't have. At 20 years old, in my first relationship, I was naïve (because it was literally my *first* relationship), I was anxious to be in love and eager to be the best thing he'd ever had. I had never experienced having to trust someone or having to be patient and forgiving. Fast-forward to present day, my husband and I have experienced some true challenges that I, if not deeply rooted in Christ, could not have lasted through. The girl that I was for my ex was timid and unsure and inexperienced. But the gap

22

years in time until I met my husband produced the woman that I am today; the one my husband chose to marry and she has been taught by the Holy Spirit how to work together and to know what *longsuffering* means.

I know you hear this often but it is the truth – singleness is not a death sentence. It's an opportunity to grow. It is your gap year(s) to become "good" as defined by God. There is no three-step prototype as to how we should carry ourselves to be considered "good". Yes, we have characteristics that make us responsible, reliable and self-sufficient. But until you are blessed with a mate and given the opportunity to get to know them and what they need, you should never claim to be a "good" husband or wife.

In a single state, we should only strive to be "good" in God's sight. But how do we know if we are going in the right direction? It is actually a lot simpler to understand than one might think. With study, reading the Creation story in Genesis 1 will explain to you how to become good in the sight of God. At the end of all the things that God brought into existence, He said it was good. Now, it is two points in that last sentence that are extremely important to understand before moving forward. The first point is this: for anything to be of any value to the earth and to God's plan, that thing must be totally formed and molded by God. Only then did God say that it was "good." And, secondly the first part "At the end of all the things..." tells us that somewhere between the beginning and the end of His creations there was a process that took place with the intent of making the creation good. The aforementioned example of how my former self could not withstand my current marriage is a prime example of what a process can transform your life into. You cannot skip, go around or abort this process because it is the essential seasoning of your life, just like the nontraditional med student. The process is what will give you the wisdom to guide your children and a story to tell the grandkids.

I know we go through the many phases of life and eventually comes the time to plan for parenthood. But, I want to tell you that even from your *own* birth you are always pregnant! My pastor often teaches a broken-down definition of the term "woman" to be "womb-man". That is, we are of man but with a womb, therefore we carry or incubate. Everything that life takes you through is part of your process to birth something out of you or as he refers to it: "pregnant with purpose"! The process is the gap year(s). The gap year(s) is/are the period during which God completely forms and molds us into the design that He imagined long before you were in your mother's womb (Jeremiah 1:5 NIV). And, during this gap period of spiritual incubation, your earthly purpose will be brought forth.

A divine purpose is the very thing you were created for. Although you may have been your parents' mistake, you are The Lord's love child and He is always intentional. As he created the innermost parts of your person, He placed in you a purpose that was specifically designed to promote His kingdom; a purpose that only *you* could fulfill. WOW! How mind-boggling is that? As of 2017 there are 7.53 billion people in the world (www.worldmeters.info/world-population); that is 7.53 billion children that God are responsible for and even still, he managed to know exactly who *you* are and assign a specific task *just* for you (*"what is mankind that you are mindful of them, human beings that you care for them?"* - Psalms 8:4 NIV). For many people the discovery of purpose takes great discipline, time and work. Ultimately, we are created to give God the glory (*"Everyone who is called by my name, whom I created for my glory, whom I formed and made."* – Isaiah 43:7 NIV). So, take a moment and think about what you do in your own life that allows you to give God glory. Do you do this often? Do you enjoy it?

You must enter the presence of God often and seek what it means to know Him and hear His voice. There can never be another you and so if you do not

27

fulfill what you were created to do, then it's one less assignment that was ineffectively carried out for God's Kingdom. Think of it this way, when we lose a loved one we cry and we share memories. Their legacy was so impactful on our lives that we continue to remember them and never can forget nor replace them. Similarly, we are all apart of God's family and every time someone doesn't answer to their purpose or abort the process to revealing their purpose, God goes to a funeral. He thinks of all the great things you would have done or taught to others. Your heavenly family mourns every decision you knowingly make that lies outside of the will of God. Rooting yourself in Him and discovering why you were created will keep you from making wrong decisions and not just with partners but in your career, your education, your family and friend circles; every aspect of your life will benefit from you finding your purpose because God is a consuming fire (Hebrews 12:29 NIV) which means that just like a wildfire, He comes to spread through, not just a few trees but the entire forest (your life) leaving you richly purified and as precious as gold.

So now you get to this point where you have allowed God to mold you. The Holy Spirit has taken over your mind and now you are saved and sanctified and (to your best ability) living a life that is pleasing unto the Lord. How do you assess your goodness in the sight of The Lord? Imagine yourself in an orchard and there are rows and rows of trees. From afar, you can't tell what kind of trees they are but upon closer inspection, you see apples hanging. You see cherries on some trees and then oranges on others. Each tree looks the same: tall, brown bark, thin branches and green leaves. The only way you could tell what kind of trees they are is by looking at the fruit. Matthew 7:20 NIV says *"Thus, by their fruit you will recognize them."* The preceding lines explain that *good* trees bear *good* fruit and that bad trees cannot produce good fruit just like good trees cannot produce bad fruit. Here, Jesus is speaking and teaches his disciples how to differentiate between the good and the bad. Good people are fruitful people. Being fruitful means that you engage in or work hard within something that produces positive results. Are you fruitful? If you are a believer of Christ, does your walk and testimony draw others to Christ? If you are a doctor, does your research provide new answers to some of life's most perplexing mysteries? If you are single, are you fulfilling and enriching your life by completing the projects and ideas that have previously

been established in you? If you are able to answer 'yes'

to any of these questions then you my friend are among

God's good fruit!

Chapter 2
Now What?

For just one moment, I'd like you to close your eyes and imagine your dream home; thinking of all the minute details from the colors of the shutters to the tiles on the floors and even to the basketball rim that is in the back drive. This is the home that you've dreamt of for your entire life and it's also the home that you've spent the majority of your years working for. My husband and I watch a lot of the home-remodeling shows on HGTV and the big hang up appears to be the square footage of every house. The more you have, the bigger your home and who doesn't want a huge house, right?

Often, these homes on the shows have to be remodeled because they're old and have been unoccupied for many years which in turn allows the elements to wear on the foundation of the home and even with over 3,000 square feet, it is no good without a sturdy foundation. Anything that could potentially compromise the safety of the occupants of the home is hazardous. The stability of any beautiful home comes from a sturdy foundation. Contractors lay brick after brick with your security (and their paycheck) in mind because they know if you're not secure, then they won't get paid. Now, think of this home as your own life. Your purpose is the foundation and though you might not expect it, *you* are the contractor. I know you may have been expecting me to say that God is the contractor of your life but the truth is, with His gift of free will, everything is up to us as individuals so you decide when to lay your bricks and how many at a time.

Everything great that is going to be brought out of your life depends on your foundation – your purpose. According to the Oxford Dictionaries, 'purpose' is defined as the reason for which something is done or created or for which something exists. Though many people want to know how to find their purpose, there is no quick and easy answer to this. If you already know what your purpose is, then consider yourself ahead of the game. However, if you do not yet know, then don't grow weary. There is still time! It often comes in the form of what you think is a hobby or pastime so we figure out what our purpose is without even knowing or trying.

When I was 11, I was faced with the difficult task of being my grandmother's caregiver as she was terminally ill with stage IV breast cancer. I developed a deep curiosity for medicine during this time – all that I knew though was that I was just taking care of my grandma; unbeknownst to me these precious moments were lying the *foundation* for the plan God would ultimately have for my life.

It's no secret how grueling it can be to pursue medicine as a career. Just the schooling admission process is gruesome enough. My husband recently shared with me that he was initially attracted to my work ethic and how focused I was on becoming a doctor. Coming from one of the hardest working and driven men that I know, I did not take this lightly. Looking back, when he first met me, I was taking 16 credit hours, working one job on campus, one job in town near the university and one job on weekends back in our hometown. I wasn't afraid to do what it took to meet my goals, even if it meant that I didn't have time to sleep.

I was never privileged to this information until we were married for a little over a year. In retrospect, for the four years that we were just friends before we dated, he was watching me, taking notes and filing them away. This gave me a whole new revelation as to what it meant when The Word outlined how Ruth was gleaning in the fields before Boaz took notice of her. She was literally working. After having followed her mother-in-law Naomi to her hometown of Bethlehem, Ruth's purpose was to care for and serve Naomi. As she worked in the field doing so, she was operating in her purpose thusly, lying the foundation for Boaz to notice her. And, he did! You see, once you have found your purpose, all you have to do my friend, is work. As previously stated, your purpose will be something that you have always done. When you finally recognize it, you will have been there before and it will be very familiar to you. The Word of God's Word tells us that our gifts will make room for us and bring us before great men (Proverbs 18:16 NIV). That is to say that operating in your gift…you purpose…will provide you with opportunities to be *noticed* by the right people at the right time.

Chapter 3
The Dusty Book

Congratulations! You've found your purpose and now this is what you will do for the rest of your life and the best part is that it is something you enjoy, something you're good at and something that allows you to praise the Lord all at the same time. Let's take a moment to be truthful with ourselves. If all you had in this life was your purpose– that is...married to the affairs of the Lord and absolutely no spouse or potential mate in sight *or* mind, could you be satisfied? "*I would like you to be free from concern. An unmarried man is concerned about the Lord's affairs – how he can please the Lord.*" (I Corinthians 7:32 NIV). Do not fool yourself. Be completely honest; would living for God alone be enough to give you that fulfilling life that you've always seen yourself living? No children, no wedding, no career...but God? The 'Believer' in us will jump for joy and say "of course, I will do anything for the Lord!" But thank God that he looks past what we wish to be and deals with us for who we truly are in that moment and still does so in love.

Thinking back to my years in college, we were taught early on to cross reference materials to gain a full understanding of a subject. This was necessary for each class but chemistry especially required different study materials. I had one chemistry textbook that I used regularly but the information that I had been looking for...that was essential to my full, circumferential understanding of IR spectroscopy, I found in the dusty book on the top shelf of the public library. The dust is suggestive of the fact that the book doesn't get used often and the location of the book (the top shelf) is indicative that it is something that you wouldn't think of right away but would really have to search through your resources to find.

Think about the purpose that you have discovered about yourself up to this point. For our example here, we will say that it is to be a counselor for suicidal prevention. According to afsp.org, suicide is the 10th leading cause of death in the U.S., ringing in 44,965 deaths per year. On average, that's 123 suicides per day. In 2016 alone, the National Survey of Drug Use and Mental Health estimated that 1.3 million adults have had at least one suicide attempt in the U.S. Now, according to the U.S. Census Bureau, on July 1, 2017, the population estimate of the US was 325,719,178 people (census.gov). The number of people who attempt or commit suicide is significantly less than the total number of the country's citizens (QUICK MATH: about 0.3991% of Americans attempt suicide per year and about 0.01380% of those who attempt are successful). Now, consider your purpose...a suicide prevention counselor. Based on our research presented here, you could deduce that the average American will probably not commit or attempt to commit suicide. But what about those who do consider suicide? As a counselor could you find contentment in knowing that you make a difference in the lives of 0.3991 % of the United States' population who attempt suicide or would you wish to mean something to the other 99.6009%? I used this example to say this: your purpose may (or may not) place you in the spotlight for many to see, but just like that dusty book, it is essential to the life of someone, somewhere; your purpose is necessary for them to gain a full, circumferential understanding of where they are headed in their own lives.

In doing so, do not be afraid to draw from your own well. Revelation 12:11 NIV explains that it is by the blood of the lamb and words of our testimony that we are able to overcome. It is impossible to pursue your purpose without sharing your testimony and this is because your testimony is the strength that will get someone else through their storm. Once your story has worked for you, it's time to make it work for another. Tell your story like someone's life is depending on it…because it is!

Chapter 4
Chordae Tendineae

In the human heart, there are thread-like structures comprised of fibrous tissues within the right and left ventricles called *chordae tendineae.* These fibers are tasked with anchoring the valves of the heart so much as to prevent valvular inversion or prolapse. More commonly referred to as "heart strings", these structures simply keep everything in the same place, which is for the betterment of our health. Now, I know you may be sitting there thinking *"is this a book of self-discovery or human anatomy?"* Well, quite parallel to these heart strings and probably more relatable to you, there are *soul ties.* Though there are a few distinctions, the bigger picture of each is generally the same. Some differences for instance are that you can physically see and touch heart strings but not soul ties. Conversely, you can feel your soul ties tugging at you and your emotions but cannot necessarily feel your heart strings keeping those valves shut. A significant point of similarity is that both the heart strings and the soul ties work to keep things in place. Now then, it becomes a matter of whether the place things are kept is life sustaining or death promoting.

As previously stated, heart strings keep valves in place which ultimately promotes a healthily pumping heart that contributes to a healthy life thus these fibers are life sustaining. However, soul ties keep you in the same place in life, which produces stagnation and eventually regression, ultimately promoting death. I know that you may have heard the term "soul tie" before but I'd like to delve a bit more into what this truly means to a single individual who is actively seeking domestic partnership and marriage.

As I am sure there are many ways, the three standards to which I hold a soul tie to be formed by is through sexual relations, through outward, physical expressions of intimacy (such as kissing) and outright verbal commitment. Before I began dating my husband, I had previously dated three guys at different times in my life whom each required a different kind of investment. Though I had not been sexually active with any of them, there was kissing involved and promises of "forever" (verbal commitment). Because each experience required investments that (at that time) I was willing to make, unbeknownst to myself, I also signed up for three soul ties that would have to be undone and permanently discarded from my life before I could reach my full protentional with the man whom God had purposed to be my husband.

The misunderstanding of whether a guy or girl is the "one" often comes from spiritual immaturity in one party and/or carnal masking in the other. Carnal masking refers to someone essentially hiding their true intentions with a person to feed what their flesh desires; simply put, telling you what you want to hear to get in your pants. Guys, you are not exempt from this. It is only often told of the guys lying to the woman to get in her pants but on the contrary I have had conversations with women who have this same mindset. This is not to say that either is okay, only to make you aware that it happens (and if she's not covering up her true intentions to get in your pants, then you may want to protect your pockets)!

Spiritual immaturity is the product of a starved relationship with Christ. Your relationship with him is strengthened by walking and talking with him daily. As your spirit matures, it's just some things you'll be able to pull apart without even having a conversation with a person – you will be able to see right through them with your "spiritual eyes". That is spiritual discernment. According to Leviticus 10:9-10 NIV, God's Word calls for us to have a sober mind so that we can rightfully distinguish between what is holy and what is common or what is clean from what is unclean. This sober mind is necessary to discern the things of the kingdom. So, what is *not* a sober mind?

Carnally, when we use the word "sober" we relate this term to alcohol use. However, when relating to the kingdom of God, "sober" refers to anything that encourages a clear and unbiased mind state. I can personally attest to charging God with the task of maneuvering through *my* mess to give me a ready word on how to get out of a situation. I Corinthians 10:13 NIV reads *"No temptation has overtaken you except what is common to mankind. And God is faithful; he will not let you be tempted beyond what you can bear. But when you are tempted, he will also provide a way out so that you can endure it."* So, while I made God responsible for rescuing me out of the mess that I, myself had created, it was already written that he provided a way of escape for me. All in all, I didn't think of going to the Word for an answer because the mess that I had created for myself involved kissing and other physical expressions of affection. Thus, I was drunken with fleshly desires, unable to operate with a sober mind and therefore I could not hear God's voice lead me to this life-saving scripture – I was caught up in a soul tie.

This is how a soul tie can keep you from living your best life. There I was caught up in one and essentially demanding that God do for me what He doesn't do for pretty much anyone. God is a god of free will. This means that when He choose us, we either can choose him right back or choose something else. He is a gentleman who will never impose His will for us *on* us and, even when we choose a road that leads to destruction, he presents us with a way out. That's just how much He loves us, that even after we break His heart, He will still show us compassion.

Women, we are naturally nurturing so everything about us begins and ends with love, care and concern. We first think that because we "just click" with a young man or that because we have had quite a few successful dates that he is tugging at our heart strings which would put them in the category of "life sustaining" as we briefly discussed earlier in the chapter. But the reality may be that he is creating and then pulling on a soul tie that, if not handled appropriately, will keep us in the same position in life. I know I can speak for myself that when I would have a good start with a guy, I would picture our entire lives in my mind from the wedding to our babies and did not understand that this was the starting point of a soul tie – my mind was clouded with thoughts that pleased my flesh so much that I didn't think to ask myself" Is this person living out God's purpose for his life?" or "Are they striving to please God in all of their ways?" which are the very first questions we should ask whether we are male or female.

Now knowing this, it is important to plainly state what will keep you from having a sober mind. Casual sex, frivolous spending with no expected return of investment, carelessly spending time without a solid purpose or goal; these kinds of things build our expectations and gives us hope in the next time it can happen when our hope should always be in Christ Jesus. God works where we create a space for him to. That is why when a person is down to their last dollar or at their wits end, He will show up in that situation and make a way as our desperation creates a space and opportunity for him to show that he is Jehovah Jireh, a sound provider.

This may be the single most important chapter of this entire book. It only takes one second to intertwine your soul with another but could take a lifetime to undo the damage. Mishandling a soul tie results in failed relationships thereafter. My Pastor always says that the enemy to your new move is an old move. That is, the enemy doesn't have to even present you with a new temptation when you've been elevated because he is willing to bet that you will still fall victim to the old temptation that he used to trap you once before. A soul tie is exactly what will keep you on the same wheel of falling victim to the temptation of the old move.

Today, I challenge you to get off that wheel and begin to decree these things (or people) out of your life so that you can live in the fullness of all that the Father has prepared for you to enjoy. One might ask, "If I cannot physically see, hold or touch a soul tie then how do I eradicate it?" By way of my own experience, these are the steps it took for me to successfully loosen…and eventually do away with a soul tie:

1. **Acknowledge the soul tie.** In anger, we may think that we don't care about the person anymore but the fact that you are angry is a direct expression of care because simply stated, when you don't care you don't get mad. Soul ties bind our emotions. When you can unexpectedly run into that person at the supermarket and you don't feel butterflies in your stomach or wonder "what am I going to

say if they see me?" then you are on the right track.

2. **Be honest with yourself: does this person align with the Word of God and further, God's purpose for your life?** Because you made it through chapter one, you now know what you were created to do and there is no second-guessing or denying it. A person who is God-sent will propel you toward that purpose while a soul tie will distract you from it or keep you too busy to tend to it.

3. **Forgive! Forgive! Forgive!** According to Matthew 6:15 NIV, if we do not forgive others, the Father will not forgive us. I know it hurts and that it's hard but we *need* to forgive the person with whom we have had soul ties. In

addition to being unforgiven ourselves,

unforgiveness results in unresolved emotions

that end up coming out against your new

partner. This is how a soul tie will keep you on

the same wheel if not properly addressed.

4. **Renounce and break the soul tie in Jesus name using the authority in Him.** A lot of the time, we do not understand the power that we are given in the name of Jesus. James 2: 19 NIV says that even demons believe that there is but one god and that they even tremble at His name! This means that pulling down those strong hold in the name of Jesus will make the demons attached to this soul tie shudder at just the sound of His name. Become one with The Word and understand the power that we have been given!

Repeat after me: *In the mighty name of Jesus Christ, I command that every soul that has been tied to mine be loosened. I bind up the attacks of the enemy and I bind up every soul tie on Earth and in Heaven and I loose emotional freedom and a sober mind on Earth and in Heaven* (Matthew 18:18 NIV).

Chapter 5

Let Freedom Ring

My mother, a life coach to both young and mature women, would often go over many of her lessons with me. She had so much valuable information and sometimes the lesson covered topics that she had either never experienced or was amid experiencing. In school, I have always graded my understanding of a subject based on the saying "if you can teach it, then you understand it." But what happens when we are called to a place of unfamiliarity and expected to perform optimally? This is just like being purposed so much as being given a clear view of where you are headed long before you arrive.

It seems unorthodox for God to give you a clean-cut purpose without a clean-cut life, right?

Wrong! This is just how God operates. He works from the endpoint of a thing to the beginning so it is not unreasonable to see the millionaire in you while you are living pay check to paycheck, the spouse in you while you are playing the field or the business owner in you while you are working a less-than-minimum-wage job. He wants to give you a glimpse of who he sees you as to motivate you to become just that. That said, if there is a beginning and an end, then obviously there must be a middle.

In chapter one I mentioned the idea of a gap year and how important it is to stick to the process. Contrary to what we learned in early grade school, two halves do not make one whole. Sure, in the world of mathematics, this is true. But when you are considering life circumstances and relationships, this is the furthest from the truth. In actuality, two halves make one broken friendship, relationship and ultimately marriage. A person should be whole before entering into a relationship and often, the missing pieces always revert to God and the person's relationship with *Him* or lack thereof. When people move ahead of God's process and place themselves into a relationship...or even worse, a marriage, they begin to fill the void with that other person and God gets left out of the equation completely.

One important factor in becoming a whole individual is confronting your past. As ugly as our former selves may have been, it is absolutely necessary to address that person before moving forward. In fact, it is impossible to move forward without addressing this person. Without doing this, our vices take root in our hearts and minds and this becomes the enemy's attempt to take control of your life. However, whether your vice was illicit sex to produce soul ties, drugs to produce an unhealthy dependency or theft to produce a fast-paced lifestyle, the strength and power of each of these perversions are no match for the strength and power of God. There is a song by Timothy Reddick called "*Free Indeed*" and I love it so much because the hook says "I choose to be free!" Every time I hear it, I am reminded of the day that I chose to be free from everything that I thought was holding me back from who God wants me to be.

If you would, travel back in time with me to about 20 years ago which would put us in the year of 1998. It was around this time that I had my first sexual encounter. Being born in 1992, this makes me 6 years old. My perpetrator was a female who was older than me by just a couple of years. This encounter was initially unwanted but not forced and sorely perverted. I say, "initially unwanted" because as this would go onto happen a few more times, each time I found myself liking it more and more and I remember even asking for it at one point. Understanding the way that *any* child's mind works, being that it was my first sexual experience, it was all that I knew and because of this, I normalized it. I got to the point where I liked my new "normal" and wanted it to happen more frequently. If you go back to your earliest bout with perversion, you will see that this is when Satan first realized God's Kingdom power within you and in that, he shot his best shot to try and corrupt you, leading you down a spiraling path that would produce everything except for holiness.

As early as 6 years old, the enemy saw my purpose and had to try and defeat me before I could even begin to live. Just as He always is, though, God was in the background and working this out of me. I thought that because I liked it, that this meant I had to be a lesbian. And, I can remember being so written with guilt and condemnation that I had to call my mother while she was at work and I told her everything that had happened from the time it began up to that point and I also told her the way that I thought I felt about it. She came up against the responsible party and her parents in my defense and reassured me that this did not mean that I had to be a lesbian. You would think that now that this was confronted, I could begin to live life as a normal little girl and move past my past. But what I did not know was that this was just Satan's way of inoculating an even greater demon into my life for me to face. Over the next 18 years, I was living a life of shame and secrecy as I struggled daily with an addiction to masturbation and pornography.

During this time, I remained a virgin as this was always pushed by my mother to save myself for my husband. But what I had come to realize was that the sexual feelings that developed at 6 years old were never dealt with; the act of bringing them on was just confronted and brought to a halt, for which I am still thankful because had it gone on, there is no telling how severe the abuse would have gotten or what kind of person I would be today. I had 18 years' worth of sexual urges that I was trying to purge myself of and I thought the only way was to masturbate. That is, until I found out that masturbation and pornography were both sins unto God. If you've ever been in a similar situation, then you know that the hardest thing to do is to live a certain way in one light and then be a completely different person once you get home. It is tiring and frustrating and above all hypocritical. Because it clearly states in I Peter 2:1 NIV that we are to rid ourselves of hypocrisy, I had to make the decision if I wanted to live a life pleasing God or live a life pleasing myself – I chose God.

On October 7, 2016, God challenged my decision and spoke to me to upload a public video onto my Facebook account and air out my "dirty laundry". (The video can be found at the following: https://www.facebook.com/taylor.ciara/videos/vb.1000 00276310809/1304068552945676/?type=3).

I took him up on that offer and uploaded a video with 'public' settings so that anyone could see my truth and not just the people who I thought enough of to call "friend". It was a very vulnerable time, my most vulnerable yet. I spoke with tears and had a knot in my gut for the duration of the video. I couldn't help but to think of what people were going to think of me. Often, we begin to believe others' hype about us that we forget the real us is who we still have to go home and face every night. In realizing this, I knew that it did not matter what anyone would think; that God has the final say and if He instructed me to reveal this about myself then just as it is written in Romans 8:28 NIV, it would all work for my good.

Today, I can talk about this without tearing up, getting nervous or feeling embarrassed or guilty. Why?

Because, just like that song by Timothy Reddick says, I *chose* to be free! Freedom became my personal declaration and I have lived by that every single day after publishing that video. This testimony is just an example of what I mean when I say you have to dig deep to confront your past in order to move forward. I don't know why God chose the timing that he did but three months later, I was blessed to become married to my husband. It was like God was sending me through his final tests and completely renewing my mind before giving me away to my husband and this was my last step.

When you're choosing life, it will always be a fight. The enemy does not want you to be great. More importantly, he does not want you to be free. His objective is to keep you bound by the experiences that has shamed you and this is where your fight begins. You cannot expect to take and be satisfied with superficial confrontation. Had I taken the easy, pity-pat way out and not addressed my true issues and causes to those issues, I know that I would not be who and where I am today. At 24-years-old, when I confronted this deep, dark issue stemming from my past I dug it up by the root and evicted the guilt that resided in my heart and mind for something that I wasn't even at fault for. This is why when I have urges today, I am strong enough to resist the enemy and as true as God's Word is, he flees every single time (James 4:7 NIV). Nobody judged me for my video. In fact, I had received many 'pats-on-the-back' for being brave enough to share something so personal as many could relate to some varying degree.

Later in my adult life, I could see and understand that she was probably only doing to me what someone had done to her. Coming from a drug-infested home, you can only guess that this was the bare minimum of the truth that she had to live out on a day-to-day basis. My heart was not hardened at her and still is not. I have forgiven her and moved on with my life. From that day up to this one, I am still choosing to please God – I haven't watched any pornographic films or masturbated and it's my heart's promise to God that I never will again.

Chapter 6
A Young Person's Guide to Self-Discovery

In this chapter, the goal is to get you to actively engaged. You've read all of the steps that is necessary to be who God wants you to be before the ring however, according to Habakkuk 2:2 we must write the vision and make it plain, for if it is not written, then it does not exist and is merely a thought or an idea. This is *your* guide to self-discovery; that means coming face to face with some things that you never gave any thought or attention to that needs to either be further developed or completely worked out of you; it is strongly encouraged that you be open and honest about each question – this is your book, your notes and your privacy with no obligation to publicly share what you've written down.

What drives you? Rate the choices below where 1 is your greatest drive and 4 is your least greatest drive.

___Money for spending or saving
___Attention from the public
___God/your spiritual beliefs
___Retirement plans
___My parents
___Your "calling" in life
___My children
___My siblings
___Myself

In the space provided below, write down what *your* purpose is:

_____

_____

_____

Are you actively walking in this purpose? If yes, how? If no, how can you engage yourself to walk in this purpose?

_____

_____

_____

Do you think that you can successfully be in a relationship/courtship without having first known your purpose? If yes, how? If no, why not?

_____

_____

_____

How many <u>real</u> relationships have you been in?

_____

_____

_____

If they have failed, why? What were you responsible for in that failing relationship? (*Here, try not to answer with focus on what the other person did. It is so easy to divert attention away from our own shortcomings especially when they aren't "as bad as" someone else's. It is important to remember that just because something seems right to us in the moment that we act, does not mean that it cannot be misperceived by another person.*)

_____

_____

_____

Have you ever been deeply hurt or abused? By whom?

_____

_____

_____

Have you ever discussed this hurt or abuse with anyone or the specific person? If no, why not?

_____

_____

_____

Have you forgiven this person or people? If no, what is keeping you from forgiveness?

_____

_____

_____

Have you ever deeply hurt or abused someone? Who and how? If yes, did they ever confront you about this? Have they openly forgiven you?

_____

_____

_____

_____

_____

_____

What is something or some things that you have been through that you do not like to talk about? Why don't you like to talk about it?

_____

_____

_____

Have you confronted the deepest, darkest issues from your past? In what ways? (*Here, it is important to know that confronting your past is something that is physically active – you can't just think about all that you've gone through and tell yourself that you are over it. True, it does begin with thinking about your experiences in your quiet time but it does not end here. As you answer this question, challenge yourself to think of who you've had a tough conversation with to truly get to the heart of some of your life's most troubling issues. If you haven't done this, write down a plan of how you intend to do so.*)

_____

_____

_____

_____

_____

_____

_____

_____

_____

Do you sometimes feel that the mistakes you've made in the past is keeping you from fully engaging in your future? If yes, how?

_____

_____

_____

_____

List those who are currently soul-tied to you? Why do you think they are a soul tie? How do you intend to break these soul-ties?

_____

_____

_____

_____

_____

_____

_____

_____

_____

_____

_____

Epilogue

When you have acquired your degrees, jobs, homes and cars but no mate, you can't help but to wonder "what is God waiting on?" I was there once. I was a fit and firm, 22-year-old college senior and working three jobs. I had my own car, housing paid for by the university and an income that was enough to support me and my family back home. I also had a steady growing spiritual relationship with God and a church home. For my age, I thought I had it all together. So, why no man? I didn't dwell on it but I'd be lying if I said it never crossed my mind. Even though the thought would creep in, it was quickly put to rest by my reality of not having time for a relationship. I can remember completely submerging myself in my service to others and loving it. Between all that I had going on, the only "free" time I had for myself had to be committed to my class work.

And then, I met my husband...or as he like to say he "found" me which is probably more appropriate since it aligns with God's Word (Proverbs 18:22 NIV). As we continued to date, God brought into my remembrance all the things I had dreamed of becoming in my lifetime: a wife, a mother, an author, a doctor, a tutor and a facilitator. I now know that cannot be all that God intended for me to be without my husband. He feeds my purpose, sees my goals when I grow weary and continues to push me towards the mark.

I discovered early on that my purpose in life is to improve the lives of others for whatever road they are taking in their lives and specifically in medicine, to be the bridge between disadvantaged black and brown communities and quality medical care. God should always be your motivation while searching for your purpose; not money, fame, social status or a romantic relationship. Sure, I was tired often but the peace and joy I felt from acting in my purpose during my college days exceeded any other feeling because I knew I was pleasing God. I was in a place of excitement, satisfaction and feeling valuable to people *and* God.

In the beginning, I stated that I do not claim to be a life coach, love doctor, match maker or anything of that sort. But, in all things, I do believe that if you find a way that works, then go with it. There is an old saying that goes "there is no need to reinvent the wheel." Why go through relational struggles, fleshly withdrawals or soul ties when you can learn ahead of time and avoid that road altogether? As I do understand that some people are just the kind who need to bump their own heads in order to get the big idea, my mother always taught me that a wise person learns from the mistakes of others.

Having followed behind so many of my mother's footsteps and lessons, I think this is why I am often referred to as the "mom" of my friend and work groups. Even though that is not what I set out to be amongst my peers and colleagues, I have come to agree that it's just who I am. I care about people and the decisions they make. The things that I say or teach about in this book are things that I've learned and lived by. They have worked for me and contributed to who and where I am today. This is why it is important that I share this so that other young people can find their road that leads to life. There is nothing in this book that I haven't done myself or that I wouldn't teach my own son. That said, this book is especially personal and invites the reader into my way of mentally processing things.

After all is said and done, it is my sincere hope that you were able to learn something about yourself in reading this book. I hope that you were able to unlock the truths about yourself that you have hidden away in your heart with no intention of ever revealing. And lastly, I hope that you are now on the road to becoming who God wants you to be before the ring. Keep growing!

<u>Connect with the Author</u>

Email: 1taylorcliddell@gmail.com

Facebook: @taylor.ciara

Instagram: @taylorcliddell

www.ingramcontent.com/pod-product-compliance
Lightning Source LLC
LaVergne TN
LVHW051427080426
835508LV00022B/3267